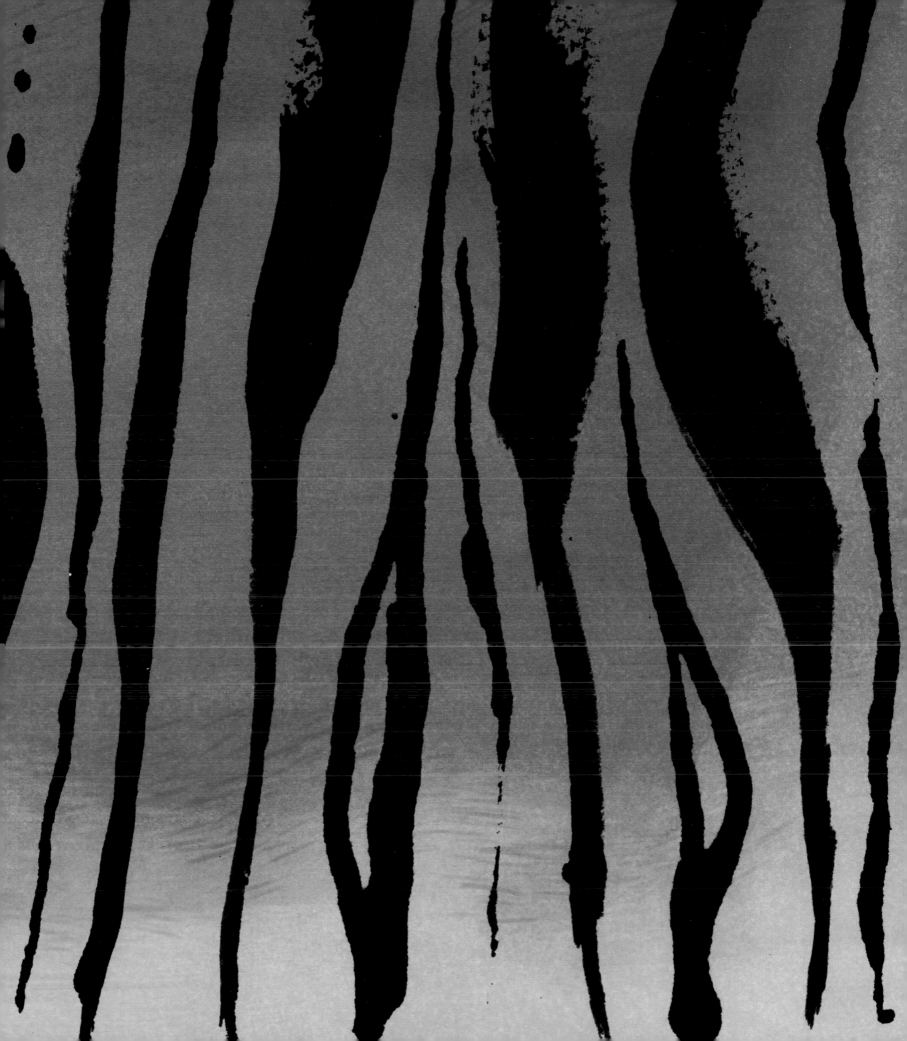

For Fin – *Louise Greig*

For Arabella, Abi, Becky, Rebecca and Faith,
who made this book so enjoyable – *Nicola O'Byrne*

First published in Great Britain 2020 by Red Shed,
an imprint of Egmont UK Limited
2 Minster Court, 10th floor, London EC3R 7BB

www.egmont.co.uk

Text copyright © Louise Greig 2020
Illustrations copyright © Nicola O'Byrne 2020

The author and illustrator have assrted their moral rights.

ISBN 978 1 4052 8782 1

A CIP catalogue record for this title is available from the British Library.

What the Animals Saw

Louise Greig & Nicola O'Byrne

RED SHED

A baby elephant sees a herd.
He weaves through giant pillars of legs, tails, trunks.
Swish, sway, swish, sway,
through a moving mountain of grey.

Mother, aunts, sisters
form a formidable army
of family to guide and protect him.

The herd is a wall of strength.

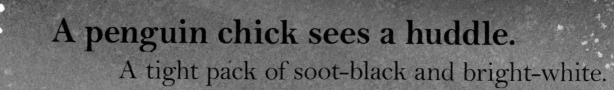

A penguin chick sees a huddle.
A tight pack of soot-black and bright-white.

Sheets of wind and snow batter and blow
above him but he is snug and warm.

The penguin parents form a brave barrier
against the cruel Antarctic storm.

**One day he will do the same
for his own chick.**

An eagle sees a hare.

From a soaring height she spots a flicker of white fur.

Is it a speck of snow?
The sharp-eyed eagle knows better.

The hare swerves in
zig-zags in a race for cover.

Who will be faster?

A gorilla sees her child.

A tiny bundle with wide open eyes
cupped in her mighty palms.

They will remain close,
   wrapped in a blanket of mountain mist,
      cuddling, climbing, clinging together for years to come.

Two hearts beating a wild drum.

An octopus sees a diver.
A sudden surge of flashlight floods her inky black shipwreck home.

What is this mask? Whose is this face?

The octopus reaches out a shy tentacle.
She is curious and gentle.

Perhaps she is saying,
'Let's be friends'.

A rhinoceros sees a rival.
A mirror of himself. A hulk of head and horn.

Each has stamped his claim on this dusty scrap of land.
Share is a word they do not understand.

They square up, glare,
        flare nostrils, snort in fury.

Only one will win the right to stay.

A rabbit sees a wolf.

A face framed with frost-stiffened fur fills the burrow with fear.

Two piercing eyes and two white fangs.
He is a chilling hunter. The rabbit does not twitch.

This time the wolf will turn
and slope off into the shadows.

Next time. Who knows?

A grizzly bear sees a salmon.
The salmon hears a rumbling belly . . .

The hungry bear is a skilful fisherman.
Great paws become scoops, claws curled to hook.

A flash and the fish will be gone.
They call this 'The Salmon Run'.

Today the bear is in luck,
but the salmon? His has run out.

A tiger sees a deer.

He prowls a silent path through the deep dense jungle,
amber eyes burning chinks in the dark.

The deer is browsing in the cool night breeze.
The tiger's black stripes look like long leafy shadows.

This big cat is clothed in a clever camouflage,
and perfectly poised to pounce.

A fish sees a duck.

First, a watery quack. *A splish, a splash!*

Then a circle of ripples.

Webbed feet thrust through the pond. *Swoosh!*

A beak dips below the surface,
as if the duck is saying,
hello, fish!

A bat sees the night sky.
The moon shines a lantern
into two waking eyes.

It's time for supper.
Soon he will stretch
soft furry wings to
swoop, dive and *flit*
like an acrobat
catching insects.

**Daytime is for sleeping,
but dusk and darkness are his friends.**

Bats are the only mammals that can truly fly. Dusk and night is when they emerge to hunt for flying insects in the air. During the day, they roost upside down in caves, tunnels, dark buildings and tree hollows.

Bears such as the North American grizzly bear hibernate in dens all winter long. They need huge reserves of fat, so they will prepare by gorging on foods such as nuts, berries, fungi and salmon.

Ducks are called waterfowl because they live in watery places. Ducks have webbed feet which work like paddles below the water, but they can also fly. Their *quack* is a very distinctive sound!

Eagles have astonishing eyesight so they can spot movement from a great height and distance. Golden eagles are majestic birds of prey found in North America, Asia, North Africa and Europe.

Elephants are the world's largest land animals and live in Africa and southern Asia. Female elephants spend their whole lives in a herd of family members. This supportive family group will work together to protect a newborn elephant.

Gorillas are the world's largest primates (a type of animal that has hands and feet). They live in groups high in the mountains and densely forested regions of central Africa.

Hares such as the snowshoe hare in North America are capable of very clever camouflage – their coats change colour from snow white in winter to brown or grey when the snow begins to melt!

Penguins such as the emperor penguin live in Antarctica on the ice and surrounding water and rear their young during the fierce winter.

Octopuses are sea creatures with eight arms and soft boneless bodies. Octopuses can squeeze themselves through small spaces. They have a wide range of techniques for camouflaging themselves including changing colour to blend in with their surroundings.

Rabbits are burrowing, plant-eating mammals with long ears and short tails. Their burrows have several entrances and resemble an underground maze. They are called warrens.

Rhinoceroses are massive plant-eating mammals found in Africa and southern Asia. They have thick armour-like skin and a large horn that grows from their snout. Rhinos look clumsy because of their giant size but they can run extremely fast!

Salmon hatch in rivers or streams. They then migrate (swim great distances) out to the ocean to live before returning years later to the place they hatched, to lay eggs.

Tigers are the largest of all the big cats and are found in Asia. The black stripes on a tiger's coat are there for a reason – they look like long shadows and offer amazing camouflage as they stalk their prey.

Wolves are carnivorous (meat-eating) animals. They are the largest of the dog family and live in packs in Europe and North America. They are expert hunters and can smell prey from long distances.